# THE WONDERFUL ROOM

## Other Books by Bryan Woolley

### Nonfiction

*Texas Road Trip*
*Where I Come From*
*Mythic Texas*
*Generations*
*The Bride Wore Crimson*
*The Edge of the West*
*The Time of My Life*
*Where Texas Meets the Sea*
*We Be Here when the Morning Comes*

### Fiction

*Sam Bass*
*November 22*
*Time and Place*
*Some Sweet Day*

### For Children

*Home Is Where the Cat Is*
*Mr. Green's Magnificent Machine*

# THE WONDERFUL ROOM

## THE MAKING OF A TEXAS NEWSPAPERMAN

BRYAN WOOLLEY

WingsPress

San Antonio, Texas

2010

First Edition
Print Edition ISBN: 978-0-916727-74-1
ePub ISBN: 978-1-60940-000-2
Kindle ISBN: 978-1-60940-001-9
PDF ISBN: 978-1-60940-002-6

Wings Press
627 E. Guenther • San Antonio, Texas 78210
Phone/fax: (210) 271-7805

On-line catalogue and ordering:
www.wingspress.com
All Wings Press titles are distributed to the trade by
Independent Publishers Group • www.ipgbook.com

Library of Congress Cataloging-in-Publication Data:

Woolley, Bryan.
The wonderful room : the making of a Texas newspaperman / Bryan Woolley. -- 1st ed.
p. cm.
"The Wonderful Room first appeared in 2006 in The Dallas Morning News"--T.p. verso.
ISBN 978-0-916727-74-1 (hardcover : alk. paper) -- ISBN 978-1-60940-000-2 (ePub.) -- ISBN 978-1-60940-001-9 (Kindle) -- ISBN 978-1-60940-002-6 (library pdf.)
1. Woolley, Bryan. 2. Journalists--Texas--Biography. I. Title.
PN4874.W6933A3 2010
070.92--dc22
[B] 2010004347

*To the memory of Ed Engledow*

# Contents

# INTRODUCTION

**One late night** after work in the 1950s, John Moran and I were sitting in the Stag Bar, drinking beer. He was the assistant city editor of *The El Paso Times* and I was its 18-year-old cub reporter. Moran was a fine editor and a lapsed Irish Catholic. Sometimes when he had had a few beers, he would become religious. The more beers, the more religious. One time he led me out of the Stag at closing time, took me home with him, woke up his wife and dragged us to the six o'clock Mass at the cathedral. A sobering experience for a Baptist kid from the wilderness.

On this night, we were discussing the *Times* and our work there, and Moran said: "Woolley, being a newspaperman is like being a priest. It's a holy calling."

During my nearly 50 years as a newspaperman, I considered my job that way, except in secular terms – finder of truth, fighter for justice, swashbuckler for freedom – rather than priestly ones. Many of the reporters and editors I've known over the years have felt the same way. What we were doing was special and essential.

So I was startled some 25 years after that night at the Stag to hear an editor at *The Dallas Times Herald* speak of the paper as "our product." It's a phrase I would hear more and more often during the rest of my career as corporations took control of family-owned newspapers and the bottom-line mentality seeped into newsrooms. We weren't so much intrepid truth-finders and swashbuckling crusaders anymore. We were "content providers" making a "product" to be marketed like Cheerios or Bud Light, complete with focus groups to tell us what the consumer wanted.

Yes, my view is romantic and old-fashioned. I know newspapers have always been a business, and sometimes even a rotten one. But always there has been that thing that John Moran called holiness, that First Amendment thing, that holding of the mirror up to the face of government and culture. No other news medium – radio, TV or now the Internet – does that. Often they just shrink and repackage what they get from the newspapers.

Now the daily papers that the country has read for the last 250 years may be fading away, to be replaced with the electronic gadgets and the video screens that most Americans now spend their lives staring into. I'm afraid our democracy is in big trouble.

This small memoir is a gathering of a few memories of my early days as a kid reporter in the cities of El Paso, Texas, and Ciudad Juárez, Chihuahua, on the Rio Grande in the 1950s, when the world and I were young and learning to be a newspaper reporter was the finest adventure I could imagine. It was a rough-and-tumble life, but yes, there was something holy about it. It sent a tingle through the mind and heart that I fear not many young people get to feel these days.

The book originally was a series that ran in *The Dallas Morning News* during the summer of 2006. My editor, Mike Merschel, had been listening patiently to my old war stories for years. He suggested that I write some of them down and offer them to our readers as a light summer entertainment. Maybe he thought that once they were in print I would stop inflicting them on him. In any case, I thank him for the opportunity to do the series and for his always careful and excellent editing of it.

I also thank *The Dallas Morning News* for its permission to reprint these words and Dean Hollingsworth's illustrations of them, and especially Editor Bob Mong and Deputy Managing Editor Lisa Kresl for their help in obtaining that permission for me.

The stories come entirely from my own memories, so there may be a few factual errors in them. Nearly all the people who could correct me have passed on, and their memory probably wouldn't be any better than mine anyway.

I'm fiercely grateful to that holy El Paso newsroom *gangito*, as some of us called it. They taught me everything.

Bryan Woolley
Dallas
October 2009

# SECTION A

## I BEGIN

**One spring afternoon** in 1953, my sophomore year at Fort Davis High School, I fell into a quarrel with my algebra teacher. She was handing back homework papers she had graded. She didn't give me one. I asked why.

"You didn't turn it in," she said.

"Yes I did."

"No you didn't."

"Yes I did."

"Are you calling me a liar?" she asked.

"If you're saying I didn't turn in my homework, you're a liar," I said.

The teacher grabbed my wrist and led me to the office of George Roy Moore, the school superintendent. As we entered, she burst into loud sobs.

"What on earth…?" Mr. Moore asked.

The teacher – a young woman not long out of college -- blubbered incoherently. One sentence, however, rang through like a gong: "He called me a liar."

Mr. Moore asked no questions. He told the teacher to return to her classroom. She departed, snuffling.

To me, Mr. Moore said, "Shut the door." Then he said, "Empty your back pockets and bend over the desk."

I remember the contents. My right rear jeans pocket held my wallet and a white handkerchief, used. The left held a black pocket comb and a folded copy of *Glory to Goldy,* the school play we were practicing. I situated myself as Mr. Moore had instructed. He took off his belt, doubled it, and whacked my backside with it exactly 20 times. "All right," he said. When I turned around, Mr. Moore was putting on his belt. Now tears glistened in his eyes, too.

His family and mine had been friends for generations. We were not-too-distant kin. Mr. Moore had gone to school with my mother. My grandmother had been his sixth-grade teacher. Now she was a member of the faculty he led.

I didn't mind the whipping much. Though I had turned in the algebra homework, I had been wrong to call the teacher a liar in front of her class. Whippings were a common punishment for schoolboys in those days. Among a boy's buddies, a whipping was even a badge of honor, evidence of badass toughness.

But Mr. Moore's tears made me ashamed. I knew they were for my mother and my grandmother, not for me.

"There's no point in your going back to class," he said. "Sit down. Let's talk."

I eased my tingling backside into the hard wooden chair beside his desk. Mr. Moore was a quiet man with calm blue eyes and prematurely gray hair, respected by everyone. He rested his elbows on the edge of the desk and laced his fingers together in here's-the-church-and-here's-the-steeple fashion. The blue eyes gazed at me for a long time. I remember the slow tick of the pendulum clock on the office wall. Finally, he said, "You're a smart boy, Bryan."

I silently agreed. In those days, I believed myself a lot smarter than I was, a self-delusion that experience eventually would correct.

"What are you going to do with your life?"

"Sir?"

"After you finish school. What are you going to do with your life? Have you thought about it?"

I hadn't. Not for an instant, unless you count my childhood yearning to be a cowboy like my Great Uncle Bryan. "No, sir."

"Why don't you be a writer?" Mr. Moore said. "I have a friend who became a writer for *Newsweek*. I've always envied him. You have the talent."

He talked for the rest of the period.

After the passage of 55 years, I still consider that conversation one of the three or four most important in my life. I wonder where I would be now and what I would be doing if that algebra teacher hadn't lost my homework and dragged me to Mr. Moore's office.

I took his advice seriously. Themes and essays had always been favorite parts of my English and history classes. Now I wrote them as I thought Robert Louis Stevenson or Mark Twain might have done. I won an honorable mention medal in an essay contest sponsored by *The El Paso Herald-Post* about soil conservation, a subject about which I knew nothing. I entered the essay competition in the district University Interscholastic League meet. I won third place. (In my junior and senior years, I would win first place at both district and regional. As a junior I also won second place at the state meet in Austin.)

About a year after my whipping, Mr. Moore approached me in the school corridor between classes and told me to come to his office immediately. My heart beat a little faster. I thought I had done nothing wrong, but I expected punishment. Why else the summons?

He offered me the same hard chair and sat down behind his desk. An envelope lay on the green blotter. He gave it to me. "Read this," he said.

It was a letter from Ted Raynor, editor of regional news for *The El Paso Times*. Mr. Raynor wanted a stringer correspondent for Fort Davis. He wondered if Mr. Moore might recommend an appropriate person.

In those days, stringer correspondents were the way city newspapers got news from the little towns in their circulation areas. Typically, a town's stringer would be the editor of the local weekly newspaper (Fort Davis had none) or some other citizen in a position to know what was happening in the place.

The stringer didn't have to be a writer. He could just gather the facts of an event, call the *Times* and dictate them to whatever reporter wasn't busy at the moment, and the reporter would organize them into a news story of the appropriate length.

At the end of each month, Mr. Raynor measured the number of column inches of news that the correspondent had contributed during the month. This was the correspondent's "string." If he had a slow month and produced only 20 inches of news, that month's string was 20 inches. In a good month, his string might be 60 inches or more, especially if he covered one of the larger towns in Mr. Raynor's territory, such as Carlsbad, N.M. or Pecos, Texas.

For each inch of his monthly string, the correspondent was paid 15 cents. For each photograph he provided, he received $2. If he provided 30 column inches of news and two photographs, for example, the *Times* sent him a check for $8.50. (The minimum wage then was 75 cents an hour.)

Of course, I knew none of this at the time.

"Would you like to do that?" Mr. Moore asked.

"Yes, sir," I said.

"Fine. I'll write to Mr. Raynor."

In a few days I received a letter from Mr. Raynor, offering me the job. The letter said I would be a "correspondent," a word that decorated my imagination with images of trench coats and fedoras and mysterious meetings in the rain. Mr. Raynor enclosed a printed sheet in which the newspaper told its stringers what kind of information they were expected to submit: Who, what, when, where, why, how, etc.

Under separate cover, Mr. Raynor sent about a dozen large yellow envelopes. The address of *The El Paso Times* was printed on them, and in big red letters: RUSH: NEWS DISPATCH. In my mind I pictured an excited editor (Mr. Raynor, probably), waving one of these envelopes and shouting: "A dispatch from Woolley! Stop the presses!"

In them I was to send Mr. Raynor news stories that weren't urgent enough to require a long-distance phone call, plus any accompanying photographs I might offer.

I brought home an old Underwood typewriter from my mother's office at the courthouse (she was the county clerk) and set it on the library table in my bedroom. I placed packets of typing paper and carbon paper on one side of it and the stack of Mr. Raynor's envelopes on the other. The Fort Davis Bureau of *The El Paso Times* was open for business.

But business was slow. In Fort Davis, a village of maybe 800 people in the isolation of the Far West Texas mountains, news was a rare occurrence. The "Fort Davis News" columns in *The Alpine Avalanche* and *The Big Bend Sentinel*, our neighboring towns' weeklies, were brief accounts of children's birthday parties, meetings of the Study Club and Sunday motor trips of Fort Davis citizens to Valentine and Balmorhea to visit relatives.

I wrote a vivid account of a chicken-house fire and our volunteer fire department's quelling of it and mailed it to Mr. Raynor. He didn't print it, so I was paid nothing. Ben Bloys, a member of a prominent local family, died and I rushed a fulsome obituary to the *Times.* Mr. Raynor slashed it to three column inches, but he ran it.

It was hidden among the back pages with the other obits. My name wasn't on it. It earned me only

45 cents. But those black words on that fragrant newsprint were mine and they were published. Thousands of people in West Texas and southern New Mexico could read them. I clipped the obit, read it over and over and over, and pasted it in a new scrapbook. Under the clip I wrote: "My first newspaper story." Next day, I took it to the courthouse to show to Barry Scobee.

Mr. Scobee was about 70 years old. In his youth he had been a lumberjack and a merchant seaman and a soldier. In the 1920s, he was a reporter for *The San Antonio Express,* but came to Fort Davis for a vacation, fell in love with the place and stayed. "After Fort Davis, all that's left is heaven," he used to say. Since he didn't know how to drive, he walked or hitched rides. In his brown fedora and brown cardigan and red bowtie he was a familiar and beloved sight about town. He was slightly deaf, but too vain to wear a hearing aid.

He was the Jeff Davis County justice of the peace and coroner. His office was up the stairs from my mother's. His job didn't require much of his time, so he wrote short stories and novelettes for *Ranch Romances, Masked Rider Western, Thrilling Western* and the other pulp magazines that made our drugstore newsstand such a gallery of blazing six-shooters every month. The pulps paid Mr. Scobee two cents a word for this work.

He also was the town historian. He had published *Old Fort Davis,* a history of the frontier Army post on the edge of town. And he was the stringer correspondent for *The San Angelo Standard-Times* and my newspaper's rival, *The El Paso Herald-Post.*

Mr. Scobee never had much money. "I never saw a coffin with saddlebags," he used to say. He was the happiest man I've ever known. Mr. Scobee welcomed me into his office. His roll-top desk and swivel chair were almost lost among wooden file cabinets, cardboard boxes, and piles of old newspapers and magazines containing his work. The narcotic aroma of musty paper permeated the gloomy air. Birdsong flowed through the open window from the trees on the courthouse lawn.

To me, Mr. Scobee always had been an elder of the town, a man who had lived a long time in the mysterious adult world that I was trying to enter. Now, suddenly, I saw him in a new way. He was what I wanted to be: a writer. He became my friend and mentor and a sort of surrogate father, even though he was older than my grandmother.

He praised my obituary, but agreed that Fort Davis didn't provide much news of interest to city newspapers, aside from the scores of our high school's six-man football games and the occasional murder trial. "Features," he said. "You have to write features."

He explained: "A feature is a story about something – a person, an event, a place – that *isn't* news. It gets into the paper not because it's important, but only because it's interesting and people will want to read it."

He rummaged through a couple of his own scrapbooks, showing me feature stories he had written over the years. They occupied far more newspaper space than the real news stories and nearly always had photographs with them. Sending variant versions of them to his newspapers in San Angelo and El Paso, whose readership didn't overlap, Mr. Scobee was building a couple of nice strings every month. During the next year, he would go through his stories with me and show me how he did them and why they worked. He read mine, and made many suggestions.

One day I received a letter from Mr. Raynor. It said he was planning a Sunday series in the *Times* about the courthouses of West Texas and southern New Mexico. Please give him a feature story about Jeff Davis County's, he said.

Mr. Scobee's files were full of the lore I needed: Fort Davis had been the seat of a huge county called Presidio, but when the railroad was built through Marfa, the larger town stole the courthouse. Then the Fort Davis people seceded from Presidio County and formed Jeff Davis County. There were tales of ranchers and cowboys, Texas Rangers, sheriffs and outlaws, soldiers, Indians, a famous jailbreak. Mr. Scobee even had good photographs of the present courthouse, built in 1910, and the adobe structure it had replaced, built in 1880.

I ran to the drugstore every Sunday to search the *Times* for my story. Week after week, Mr. Raynor was celebrating some other county: Lea, Dona Ana,

Lincoln, Culberson, Hudspeth, Brewster. Where O where was Jeff Davis?

Then on Sunday Oct. 17, 1954, I opened the *Times,* and there was, spread across the top of almost an entire inside page, this headline: "Ft. Davis Has Been County Seat Of Two Counties." And below it, the most beautiful words I have, even to this day, ever seen in print: "By Bryan Woolley."

Mr. Scobee was as proud of my first byline as I. He carried a clipping in his pocket and showed it to anyone who would look.

I ransacked his mind and files for subjects for more features. He and I roamed the old fort and old cemeteries together. I drove, of course. He climbed Dolores Mountain with me, an amazing feat for a man of his age. We sat in his office and talked for hours.

I wrote about a still-living old soldier who had served at the fort in the 1880s. I wrote about Uncle Billy Kingston, who as a child had met George Scarborough, the man who shot John Selman, who shot John Wesley Hardin. My story about the 60th wedding anniversary of Mr. and Mrs. Jessie Merrill, pioneer ranchers, made Page One, with picture, another proud Sunday for Mr. Scobee and me.

In his capacity as coroner, Mr. Scobee also introduced me to death.

One morning I rode in the backseat of the county's only police car, bouncing over a narrow, rocky road. In the front seat, Sheriff Tom Gray and Mr. Scobee were talking as though it was a normal day, but I was speechless. I had never seen a corpse.

We were headed toward a ranch headquarters where a cowboy had shot and killed an illegal Mexican national who had broken into the house.

I remember the dead man's black hair, full of dust and moving slightly in the breeze.

The *Times* ran a few paragraphs, but no byline. In those days, a reporter's name didn't appear on every story he wrote. A byline was a gift from the editor for a job he considered well done. During my time as a stringer, my byline appeared only on a few feature stories.

In the spring of 1955, two years after my conversation with Mr. Moore, I was to graduate from Fort Davis High. As the eldest child of five, supported by two women on small salaries, I would thenceforth be on my own, loose in the world.

I wanted to go to college, but would have to find a job to do it. I drove to El Paso and introduced myself to Mr. Raynor, who introduced me to Bill Latham, the managing editor. I urged Mr. Latham to hire me. I would be a copyboy, anything. He said he had no job to offer. I drove home, deeply sad for all the 200 miles, fearful for my future.

A week later, a letter arrived from Ed Engledow, the *Times* city editor. I hadn't met him. I had never heard his name.

His letter read: "Mr. Latham has gone into the hospital for a hernia operation. In his absence, I'm acting managing editor. If you can get back here before he returns, I'll give you a job."

I packed my suitcase.

# SECTION B

## THE WONDERFUL ROOM

**The room into** which I stepped on that June afternoon in 1955, a couple of months shy of my 18th birthday, was everything my imagination wanted it to be. There were six rows of reporters' desks with typewriters on them, arranged two to a row. At several desks, reporters already were writing, their neckties loosened, one even wearing a fedora, cigarettes dangling from their lips, smoke curling blue into the fluorescent lights. The heady aromas of ink and newsprint and coffee mingled with the cigarette smoke. Typewriters and Teletype machines chattered, telephones rang, reporters and editors laughed and shouted at each other.

At the left end of the newsroom was a large desk shaped like a horseshoe, with another desk jammed against it, perpendicular to the horseshoe's closed end. The space inside the horseshoe, I would learn, was called the "slot." There Mr. Latham (when he returned from his surgery) would sit most nights, ramrodding the making of the next morning's newspaper. To Mr. Latham's left sat Raynor, editing his regional stringers, and to his right sat the wire editor, Bill Cook, handling dispatches delivered by the Teletype machines of The Associated Press, The United Press and The International News Service. These editors' work places were the "rim."

The desk protruding from the horseshoe was the city desk, Engledow's place. He ran the reporters. Along one wall were the sports desk and the Sunday desk, little domains on their own, and at the opposite end of the room from the slot, the women's desk.

On a table behind the slot, a police radio mumbled metallically and spewed bursts of static. Near it a pneumatic tube system rose into the ceiling. A copyboy was rolling up stories for the early edition, stuffing them into cylinders and shooting them through the tube to the composing room downstairs.

The floor trembled under my feet. The presses in the basement were roaring out the day's last edition of the *Herald-Post*, and the *Times* cycle was getting underway.

Although intense rivals, the two newspapers occupied the same Spanish-style building at Mills and Kansas Streets. Both newsrooms were on the third, top floor. They shared the advertising and circulation departments, and used the same wire room, composing room and presses. But the Scripps-Howard chain owned the *Herald-Post,* which published in the evening, and a local man, Dorrance Roderick, owned the *Times,* which published in the morning.

A sallow, black-haired man, skinny as I and much shorter, saw me standing awkward inside the swinging doors. He rose from his first-row reporter's desk and sauntered to me, his dark eyes squinting. "Yes?" he said.

His name was Lynwood Abram. He was one of the best reporters. "I'm looking for Mr. Engledow," I said.

"Hey, Ed!" Abram said. "The mullet's here!"

"What's a mullet?" I asked.

"A useless fish," Abram said, and walked away.

Engledow was at Mr. Latham's place in the slot, rolling up his sleeves, preparing for the night's work. He was even darker than Abram, with even sharper black eyes, American Indian looking. His mouth seemed fixed in a permanent sneer.

"You're Woolley," he said.

"Yes, sir."

"You want to be a newspaperman."

"Yes, sir." I was nervous, trying not to show it.

"Well, you beat Latham back." Mr. Engledow laughed, a high-pitched "hee-hee-hee" that didn't match his speaking voice. "But he was right. There aren't any job openings here."

My heart made a fist.

"I've made up one," he said. "Come on."

He escorted me about the newsroom and introduced me to everyone who had arrived for work so far. Art Leibson, the city hall reporter, and Steve Barker, the courthouse reporter, both of them old hands. They glanced at me without curiosity, grunted and returned to their frantic two-finger typing. The other reporters were in their late 20s and their 30s. Nancy Miller was friendly, and Ralph Lowenstein, and Ramon "Pete" Villalobos, and the librarian, Baltazar Alvarez, a kind man.

Raynor, a frail, gray-haired, gray-faced man wearing a green eyeshade, muttered as if I were a stranger. I would learn he rarely spoke to anyone except his stringers, and to them only on the phone. I would learn that he had liked my Fort Davis features so much that he suggested Engledow hire me. He never told me he liked them. Raynor's behind-his-back nickname in the newsroom was "the gray ghost."

Engledow led me down the hallway to the photo studio and introduced me to the only *Times* photographer, Jorge Bate. He was a small, nervous bantam type who wore cowboy boots and huge green aviator sunglasses and a brown cloth cap like the one Hemingway wore fishing.

"You'll be Jorge's assistant," Mr. Engledow said. "He'll teach you to develop film and print pictures. He'll teach you how to use a camera. You'll work four hours a day. You'll be paid a buck an hour." (The minimum wage.) "If something better comes up, we'll see about it."

He departed, leaving me in Bate's charge. Bate whined at length about how overworked he was. It was about time he got some help, he said. He showed me around his darkroom, then invited me home with him for dinner.

Bate and his wife lived in a tiny apartment in the basement of an old brick building not far from the newspaper. We had a beer while Mrs. Bate prepared a meal of fried chicken, mashed potatoes, biscuits and iced tea. She was a young, attractive Mexican woman. She spoke not a word of English. Bate spoke no Spanish. Neither did I, beyond "por favor" and "gracias."

It was an odd evening.

Bate taught me how to develop his film and use the enlarger to make prints from the negatives.

That's what I did from 2 to 6 p.m. every day. In the mornings I took summer classes in English and history at Texas Western College. When my workday ended, I studied at the public library until it closed, then rode a bus from San Jacinto Plaza to the little house beyond Mt. Franklin, near Fort Bliss, where my mother's cousin, her husband and two children lived. I paid $10 a week for their spare bedroom and breakfast. The late-night buses out Dyer Street were full of drunk, puking GIs getting back to base.

The day Mr. Latham returned to work, I was the first thing he saw. I was wearing my rubber darkroom apron and laying some photographs in the wire basket on the city desk. While he took off his hat and coat and donned his green eyeshade and sleeve garters, his face got redder and redder. He said not a word to me.

One afternoon in mid-July Chuck Whitlock, the sports editor, came to the darkroom. "Hey, Woolley," he said. "We could use some night help on the desk. Taking calls from stringers, writing shorts about ladies golf tournaments and softball games and the like, writing heads. You interested?"

The job was 20 hours a week, 7 to 11 p.m., at a dollar an hour. For the remainder of the summer and most of the fall, I worked in Bate's darkroom in the afternoon and on Whitlock's sports desk at night.

Then I got fired.

# SECTION C

## MY CAREER IN PERIL

**Quitting and** getting fired were common events in newsrooms in those days. Many reporters and copy editors were itinerant laborers who wandered the country, working in one town and then another, their wanderings often depending on the weather. They went north in the summer and south in the winter.

Newspapermen also tended toward volatile tempers, which were sometimes fueled by alcohol, and they favored spur-of-the-moment ultimatums. If a reporter got furious with an editor, he quit. If it was the editor who blew up, he fired the reporter. The departing scribe was supposed to give or get two weeks notice, but often decamped before the deadline.

Jimmie Cotten, a police reporter, once got so furious that he batted out a long, sulfurous resignation letter. Damn the two weeks notice, it stated; Cotten's departure would be immediate. He thrust his letter into Mr. Latham's hand just as Latham was distributing our Christmas bonus checks. Latham declared that since Cotton was no longer an employee, he would get no bonus. And he didn't.

Some bilious newspapermen would return to El Paso and get hired again after six months or a year in Albuquerque or Tucson or San Antonio. Cotten did that. Others disappeared forever.

I had just arrived for work one Monday. Chuck Whitlock said, "I want to see you in the morgue."

The morgue was the small chamber off the newsroom that contained file cabinets full of old newspaper clippings and photographs. It was the domain of Balta Alvarez, the librarian, who filed and found things for us. The newsroom coffeepot was in the morgue. The morgue also was where serious private conversations were held.

Balta could sense whenever such a conversation was about to happen and would disappear. A reporter entering the morgue for a cup of coffee, seeing a private conversation in progress, would leave with empty cup. To be summoned to the morgue was bad. Private conversations there were rarely happy.

Whitlock weighed close to 300 pounds. He had wavy reddish hair and sported a city slicker mustache. He looked a little like the actor William Conrad. He was sweating. I saw he didn't like what he was about to do.

"I've got to let you go," he said.

"Go?" I said.

"I'm giving you two weeks notice," he said. "You're fired."

On the previous Friday night, he reminded me, I had taken a call from a stringer in New Mexico who was reporting his town's high school football game. It was an important game, maybe a district championship. I took notes, wrote the story, wrote a headline for it and sent it all down the tube to the composing room. Nobody but I had read the story before it appeared in the newspaper.

"You left out the damn score," Whitlock said. "You wrote the whole damn story and never mentioned the damn final score. Half of New

Mexico is jumping down my throat."

I apologized. I said I would be more careful. I would do better.

"Writing a story about a ballgame and leaving out the damn score, that's unforgivable," he said. "You're fired. Two weeks notice."

He poured himself a cup of coffee and left. Balta reappeared. He shook his head sadly.

The newsroom was hellish on Fridays in the fall. Every stringer in West Texas and southern New Mexico was delivering the results of his local ballgame. Every reporter and editor worked Fridays and was expected to pitch in. We sports people – Larry Johnson and Walt Switzer besides Whitlock and me -- inhabited the deepest pit of this football hell. We took more calls than anybody, wrote nearly everything, gave the stuff a quick read, put headlines on it and shipped it all downstairs. Of course mistakes crept in. Only one was unforgivable. I had made it.

Subsequent evenings on the sports desk were nearly unbearable. My presence embarrassed Whitlock, Johnson and Switzer. They averted their eyes from me. They spoke to me only when necessary, and then in an embarrassed mutter. They didn't hate me. They just wished I wasn't there.

So did I. Less than six months into my newspaper career, I was a failure. Halfway into my first full semester in college, I probably would have to drop out. I visited the Navy recruiter. I went to work that day and announced to Whitlock and the others that I was joining up. Maybe I would go to Japan.

The night before I was to sign my Navy papers, Whitlock called me into the morgue again. He poured me a mug of coffee, shot me his serious William Conrad look and said, "Woolley, you've been doing a damn good job lately. We'd like you to stay. I was in the Navy. It's no damn good."

Of course I would stay.

Later that same night, Ed Engledow called me into the morgue. "I talked to Latham," he said. "We're giving you a five-dollar raise."

# SECTION D

## FAMOUS PEOPLE I USED TO KNOW

A **few months** after Chuck Whitlock unfired me, a city desk reporter blew up and quit. He stormed out the swinging doors and jabbed the elevator button like it was Engledow's eye. Before he reached the street, I had asked Bill Latham for his job. Mr. Latham was in the slot, pulling on his sleeve garters. He squinted from under his eyeshade, studied my face a long time. "All right," he said. "I'll tell Chuck and Jorge you're moving over Monday." Just like that. Suddenly I was a real reporter.

A young Oklahoman named Bill "Monty" Montgomery worked police and was the best reporter on the paper. I worshipped him. Within a few months I was covering cops on his days off.

The rest of the time I was a general assignments reporter, although we didn't use that term. We also didn't use the term "journalist," a word then coming into fashion among college-educated members of the craft. "A journalist," said Ed Engledow, "is just a newspaperman looking for a job." We were reporters. We wrote about everything.

In the years since, I have come to realize how lucky I was to get some of the assignments I did. To the green kid that I was, some were frightening. I knew so little. But to show my fear would invite ridicule from the other reporters. They would see me as "the mullet," the useless fish that Lynwood Abram had called me when I arrived.

The first famous person I interviewed was Conrad Hilton, the hotel tycoon. He owned a large hotel in downtown El Paso and was a director of the city's largest bank. He flew in a few times a year for board meetings. He also was a buddy of our publisher. So every time Hilton came to town, some *Times* reporter had to interview him.

All the reporters had done the Hilton story at least once and thereafter dodged the assignment if they could. The newest guy got stuck with it.

The elevator zipped me to Hilton's penthouse. A polite black man in a white waiter's coat ushered me into the living room, where stood a huge bar. The president of the bank was standing behind the bar, and Hilton was perched on a barstool. Their faces glowed like Christmas trees. They were swacked.

"What's your pleasure?" the bank president asked me.

"Bourbon and water," I said.

He gave me scotch and soda.

I asked Hilton what he thought of President Eisenhower's economic policy. He said he liked it. I shot a picture of him and the bank president shaking hands and left.

I had a drink – I think several – with Ty Cobb, too. The great hall of famer had come to town to make a speech to the kids on Little League opening day. He and a quart of vodka were holed up together at the Gateway, a plain but clean little hotel on Texas Street. He told me baseball stories. He said he never intentionally spiked anybody when he slid into those bases, as many had accused. True, he said, he sometimes sat in front of the dugout and sharpened his spikes with a file, but just to intimidate the opposing team. He never hurt a fly, he said.

Years later, I read that Ty Cobb was a nasty, violent, racist man. But on that day he was a great and funny storyteller and I was a happy and slightly tipsy listener.

One Sunday afternoon, Engledow sent me to Liberty Hall to interview Andrés Segovia, the great Spanish classical guitarist, who was rehearsing with the El Paso Symphony Orchestra for their impending performance together. Hitherto, the only guitar playing I had heard was the likes of Les Paul and Chet Atkins on the radio and mariachis and flamencos in Juárez. I had heard almost no classical music of any kind.

Segovia, an older man, was slouched in one of the audience seats, listening to the orchestra rehearse another piece, waiting for his turn. He was smoking a pipe. So was I. Pipe-smoking was something "college men" did in those days. Segovia and I compared and discussed our pipes. His was an elegant, expensive Dunhill from England. Mine was a $2 Kaywoodie from Sun Drug Store. Segovia pretended to admire it.

He gave me a ticket to his performance. My seat was in the front row. On the night of his performance, when he walked onto the stage, he winked at me.

Another night, Engledow gave me a slip of paper with "Louis Armstrong" and "Coliseum" scribbled on it. "Grab a camera and get a little feature," he said.

Small round tables with white cloths and candles covered the basketball-court floor. A huge white sheet draped tent-like from the ceiling, probably meant to keep the music from bouncing about the Coliseum's cavernous depths. Dressed-to-the-nines couples, black and white and brown, were dancing.

A black, sweaty man was fronting the orchestra, grinning, holding a golden trumpet with a white handkerchief. I knew how great he was. I had heard him on the radio and owned a few of his records. I had been a trumpet player at Fort Davis High School.

I made my way among the dancers, holding my big Speed Graphic camera before me like a shield. By the time I reached the stage, Armstrong was playing. I stood at the stage edge, my eyes level with his shoes. When he stopped, I reached out and tugged on his trouser cuff. He bent forward and cupped his ear with his hand.

"*El Paso Times,*" I said. "May I ask you a few questions?"

"OK, man," he said. "Next break." He pointed to an empty table near the stage that apparently was reserved for him. I shot a couple of pictures. My big flashbulbs exploded like lightning. I sat down and listened.

At the break, Armstrong sat down, too, and grinned at the skinny white boy. He took a pack of cigarettes from his pocket and offered me one. He took one, too, and lit both with his lighter. A waiter brought us drinks, scotch and water, I think.

He said, "What can I tell you?"

I don't remember what I asked. I don't remember what he told me. I remember that for 15 minutes I was in the presence of a god.

# SECTION E

## THE BURGLAR

**Whenever** I substituted for Monty Montgomery on the police beat, I hung out late at night in the office of the captain of detectives. Unlike many cops, the night captain liked reporters, at least Monty and me. I could monitor the police radio there, and the captain would let me use the phone. On slow nights, he would sit at his desk and drink coffee with me and tell jokes.

Round midnight, a jail trusty would come in to empty the wastebasket and mop the floor. It was usually a different trusty every night. But then the same trusty showed up several nights in a row. He was a skinny middle-aged white man with graying hair who walked with a limp. One night when the captain was out, this man and I fell into conversation while he was mopping.

He told me his name. I don't remember it. I'll call him Bob. I don't remember why he was in the El Paso County Jail, either, but he said his profession was burglary. He had first gone behind bars when he was 14, he said, and had spent more than half his life in the state prisons of Arkansas, Oklahoma, New Mexico and Texas. One time when he was trying to swing aboard a freight train, he missed his grab and fell. The train ran over his foot and severed his toes. He hated the limp because it made it easy for cops to spot him, and he could no longer run from them.

"When I get out of here, I'm going straight," he would say. "I'm going to make something of myself." He said that every night, deeply sincere. He talked about hoboes, crooks and convicts he had known, as someone might remember cousins or schoolmates.

Next time I went home to Fort Davis, I looked up my grandmother's newspaper clippings about the 1932 murder of my grandfather, Audie Gibson, a Hamilton County deputy sheriff. Two robbers attacked him on a snowy night and shot him with his own gun. They were sentenced to life in the Texas pen. I wrote down their names, and next time I saw Bob I asked if he knew them.

"Yeah," Bob said. "They're down in Huntsville. Killed a deputy in Hamilton County."

"That deputy was my grandfather," I said.

"Oh. Sorry to hear that." He sounded sincere, not even awkward about it. Like a preacher or undertaker.

"So they're still alive."

"Yeah. They're good baseball players."

When Monty got back from vacation and returned to the police beat, I told him about Bob. He was even more fascinated by the burglar than I was, and believed Bob really did want to go straight and make something of himself.

Monty had a talk with Gill, who owned the Stag Bar, where the newspapermen hung out after work. Gill, a huge, redheaded Viking of a man, was tough, generous and funny, the perfect host for a joint inhabited nearly entirely by reporters, cops and GIs. Monty told Gill about Bob's criminal life and his prison record. He asked Gill to give Bob a job after he got out of jail.

If there were two more cynical guys in El Paso than Monty and Gill, I never met them. But, like many hardened reporters and bartenders, they each held a secret hope that, given the chance, fallen men want to become good. Despite the risk he knew he was taking, Gill gave Bob a job.

It was much like being a trusty. Bob mopped the floor, wiped the bar, washed beer glasses, lugged the garbage out to the alley. Whenever Monty and I were in the Stag, Bob would slide into our booth and tell us how grateful he was for the break that Gill and Monty and I had given him, although I hadn't anything to do with it.

"This is the berries, boys," he would say. "No more jail for me. I'm going to make something of myself." Then he would tell us what an easy thing it would be to break into the bank next door, and how he would go about it.

As we walked along the sidewalk one day, he pointed out various ways he could get into any business on Mills Street in less than five minutes. The best time to break into a department store, he said, is at closing time, while the employees are getting ready to go home.

A couple of weeks after he hired Bob, Gill discovered the old pickup that he kept parked in the alley wasn't there. He went to unlock the Stag's back door and found the lock was broken. Inside, the coin boxes of the jukebox and the pinball machine had been jimmied and the nickels were gone. Gill called the cops, who made a lot of fun of him.

After he closed for the night, Gill went home and learned Bob had broken into his apartment and made away with all his clothes. Who knows why? Gill was three times Bob's size.

Somebody in New Mexico got suspicious about all those nickels Bob was spending. He was arrested and returned to El Paso. Monty and I visited him in jail.

"I'm sorry I let you boys down," Bob said. "I can't make a go of the outside. It's too hard."

# SECTION F

## BODIES

**Jimmie Cotten** was an excitable guy with a big ego. He thought he was a gift to newspapers and women and spent a lot of time looking into a pocket mirror he carried and combing his wavy brown hair. He was a snappy dresser. He was a braggart. He thought every story he wrote was the best of the day and should be on the front page with his byline on it. Nobody in the newsroom liked him much, especially Engledow and the women, but Cotten didn't know or didn't care.

One night he was covering cops for Monty. Around midnight he burst through the swinging doors and dashed for his typewriter, shouting: "Is mad-dog hyphenated!"

That homicide wasn't any more notable than the three or four Monty might cover in the course of a month or the one or two that I might. Other reporters covered a killing from time to time, too, but Monty was the regular police reporter and I was his most frequent substitute, so we got most of them. And since I used the Speed Graphic with more ease than Monty did, I often was sent along as photographer to his more photogenic crime scenes. Most homicides rated maybe three or four inches of type. Only a few were worth a picture, but I shot a lot just in case Engledow decided he wanted them.

Almost two years had passed since I rode with Mr. Scobee and Sheriff Gray to that Jeff Davis County ranch to look at the dead Mexican, my first corpse. In that time I had become accustomed to seeing dead bodies. So used to it I worried that something was wrong with me. At first, the cops at a homicide scene would watch out the corners of their eyes to see the kid's reaction to the horror and the mess. I tried not to show any. I pretended the bloody sight had no more effect on me than on the detectives. After a few months, I wasn't pretending. Dead people didn't bother me. Was that natural? I worried about it.

But 50 years later, some of those dead still inhabit my mind, so maybe I wasn't so tough as I thought I was.

Two little black boys, 8 or 9 years old, stole a couple of cigarettes from their mother and went to the tarpaper privy behind their home to smoke them. The boys somehow set the privy afire. The tarpaper stuck to their bodies like napalm. The flames killed them in a few terrible seconds. The stench of burnt flesh and melted tar has never left me.

Those little boys were part of my worst week on the police beat, when I had to look at 11 corpses in five days.

One was a suicide on the Mesa Street side of San Jacinto Plaza. A man, well dressed in suit, necktie and overcoat, was standing on the sidewalk among the pedestrians on a cool evening and pulled a revolver from his pocket, stuck the barrel in his mouth and pulled the trigger. A crowd gathered to gawk. The first cop on the scene, trying to control the spectators while waiting for detectives to arrive, took off his own coat and draped it over the dead man's head. I shot his picture like that. The pool of blood that oozed from under the coat reflected the streetlamps.

I mentioned the cop and his kind deed in my story. Monty had taught me the way for a reporter to make a cop a friend was to put his name in the paper. So whenever I wrote about a shooting or a bar knifing or a bad car wreck, I stuck in the names of the responding officers and sometimes quoted them. The cops appreciated it. Fire fighters, too. Many of them kept scrapbooks.

Sometimes when I was hanging around the police station and a couple of cops would be leaving to respond to a call, they would come find me. "Hey, Woolley," they would say. "You want to ride?"

Riding with cops, siren screaming, lights flashing, was a thrill I didn't care for, especially when the driver's partner would slip into the back seat and leave the front passenger seat to me. The El Paso cops had been taught to drive by bats out of hell. They flew at 60 or 70 miles per hour through heavy traffic on dark streets, their lights and sirens scaring the bejesus out of every citizen within sight and hearing. I braced my feet hard against the floor and one hand hard against the dash to avoid sliding across the seat and banging into the driver, thus causing him to lose control and pilot the car into oncoming traffic, killing us all. I was certain it would happen eventually. I would die in a traffic crash with a cop driving.

I had seen it happen often enough without a cop at the wheel. In the '50s, an era of big V-8 engines and no seatbelts or airbags, a multiple-fatality car wreck was more gruesome than a murder. The impact sometimes would drive the engine into the front seat. The steering column would crush the driver's chest. His date on the passenger side would slam her head against the steel dashboard. Her skull would shatter like a china teacup.

In a crash that sticks in my mind, three people died. What makes it memorable to me is the piece of scalp and some blond curls stuck with blood to the dashboard and the bits of brain spattered here and there. The kids had been drinking.

That same week, on a bright, sunny afternoon, an ambulance was carrying a woman either to a hospital or home from one. The driver guessed he could get across a railroad track before an oncoming freight train reached the crossing. He was wrong. The locomotive slammed broadside into the ambulance. The driver, the attendant, the patient and pieces of the ambulance were strewn along the track for a quarter of a mile. The train engineer was distraught, but there was nothing he could have done.

I remember another man only because of his odor. A room clerk or a maid found him in his room in a seedy downtown hotel. He had been there a few days with his window closed in the hot El Paso summer, dead. I'm sure the police found out who he was and why he died, but I don't remember. His clothing looked like a salesman's. I didn't even enter the room. I looked through the door, saw a cop retch, and left.

Which brings me to the floater. Floaters were common in El Paso. Somebody would kill a man and dump him in the Rio Grande. Fish would eat his eyeballs and other tender parts. After a few days, his body would start to decompose and fill with gas and rise to the surface. Somebody would find it and report it to the authorities, or maybe not.

The cops figured this particular floater had been in the water about two weeks. His eyeballs were gone. His body was swollen to at least twice its normal size. His skin was dark gray. There was no way of telling even what race he was. He was barefoot, but otherwise fully clothed. Some toes were missing. Since he had swelled up so, his clothing fit him more snugly than his own skin used to. The cops would have to cut it off him. One of the detectives, as a dare, I think, asked if I would like to watch. I said sure.

They brought the floater, still wet from the river, into a funeral home and laid him on a long, low table. Two detectives, one on each side, began cutting at his shirtsleeves with pocketknives. Sometimes tiny bits of rotten flesh would come loose with the cloth. After a few minutes, when they needed air, the cops stood up and stepped away, and their partners worked with the knives for a while. All the while, the four detectives told each other dirty jokes. Whenever they laughed, they looked at me, and I would laugh, too.

# SECTION G

## I AM PROMOTED

**Ed Engledow** called me into the morgue, where all private conversations were held. I had been fired and unfired there not many months ago, so I was nervous. Engledow laid his hand on my shoulder and gave me a sneer that tried to be a smile.

"I'm giving you a promotion," he said.

I was 19 years old. I had been a reporter for just a year. "A promotion?" I asked.

"Assistant Sunday editor," he said. "Second-in-command of the Sunday Department."

The "Sunday Department" was two desks jammed together in a corner of the newsroom. The Sunday editor, Buddy Halloran, sat at one desk, and his assistant, Mel Geary, sat facing him. Their job was filling the inside pages of the next Sunday paper with canned feature stories from the wire services and the syndicates.

They sat hour after hour, week after week, editing the stuff, marking it into the Sunday dummies and sending it to the composing room. Then they had to read all the page proofs. Buddy and Mel rarely spoke to each other. They almost never left the building. They lived in their own tiny world. The rest of the staff ignored them.

Now Geary had won his release. He was about to move to the city desk as Engledow's underling. I was the sucker designated to replace him.

"I don't want that job," I told Engledow.

"A $5 raise goes with it," he said.

"I'm a reporter. I don't want a desk job. Especially that one."

Engledow's black eyes glinted. He was angry. "I'll give you a choice, son. Take it or leave."

"Take it or leave the *Times?*"

"Yeah."

I was angry, too. "I'll leave," I said.

"Two weeks notice," he said.

The word spread quickly. Some reporters resented what had happened to me. Some feared they might be tossed the Geary job. Engledow went into a black funk. He snarled and spent a lot of time staring into his coffee, which he laced from time to time from a bottle of bourbon in his drawer.

This time I didn't think of joining the Navy. I was a professional now. I set out to find a new job as a writer. The evening *Herald-Post* was out of the question. Their reporters worked mornings, while I was in class at Texas Western. I phoned every radio station. They said they didn't have reporters. Their disk jockeys just ripped the news off the Teletype and read it into the microphone.

"You've a good voice," said the manager of KHEY, the hillbilly station. "You could be a disk jockey." He offered to audition me. I said no.

I don't remember why I didn't call the TV stations. I didn't see much TV, so maybe I never thought of it having news.

During a lonely lunch at the Oasis Restaurant, the bright-idea light flashed in my head. I slipped a nickel into the pay phone and called Ed Hochrein.

Hochrein was one of maybe a dozen public relations people who came to the *Times* every day to drop news releases into a basket on Engledow's desk. The releases were long, fulsome things extolling whatever company or charity or club or big shot the PR man had been paid to promote. From time to time, Engledow would grab a handful of them, drop them on an idle reporter's desk and say, "Give me a couple of grafs on these." So the PR guy's glowing pages would appear in the paper as a few lines of plain facts. They were filler.

Some PR men would hang around and gossip and joke with the reporters and deskmen. Engledow enjoyed some of them. But he hated Ed Hochrein. I never knew why. His hatred was complete and unebbing.

Hochrein feared Engledow. But his livelihood depended on getting his clients' names into the city's largest newspaper, so he stepped through the swinging doors, dropped his releases into the basket and tried to withdraw before Engledow shot an insult at him.

I phoned Hochrein and asked him for a job.

There was a pause on the line. Then he said, "Really?"

"Engledow fired me."

I swear I could hear him smiling. "How much do they pay you over there?" he asked.

"Sixty a week," I said. It's what I would have been paid had I accepted the promotion.

"I'll pay you that," Hochrein said. "Can you start Monday?"

"You bet," I said. "Thank you."

I arrived at the *Times* at four o'clock. It was a busy part of the day. The daytime beat men were batting out their stories, the night people were drifting in. I stood in front of Engledow's desk and said loudishly, "I don't need two weeks notice. I start a new job Monday."

"Doing what?" Engledow asked.

"Writing PR for Ed Hochrein."

He went slack-jawed. So did everybody. The wire machines' chatter punctuated a long silence.

"Why the hell you doing that?" Engledow said. "You're a goddamn newspaperman!"

"I got to have a job," I said.

He picked up a piece of copy and swiveled his chair to talk to the wire editor. Back to work. Our conversation was over.

As the night deepened, his funk grew darker.

Near one o'clock, when the last of us were quitting for the night, Engledow called me into the morgue. "If you turn down Hochrein, you can stay. I'll give you the 5-dollar raise."

"OK," I said.

Then he and I went to the Stag and had a beer.

# SECTION H

## JUÁREZ

JUÁREZ
LA

**El Paso** was a small city, maybe 200,000 people, but being a reporter there wasn't at all like working in Albuquerque or Denver. Even Dallas or Houston didn't offer the drama and adventure that El Paso did. For Juárez lay across the river.

Juárez was bigger than El Paso but didn't look it. It still resembled the tacky old adobe town where Pancho Villa fought three battles during the Mexican Revolution. But it was in a foreign country and spoke another language, which made it exotic to tourists and young GIs. And it was a pit of danger and sin, which made it irresistible.

In the '50s, if you didn't have much money or the right connections, Texas was a hard place to get wicked. Bars couldn't legally serve hard liquor, only beer and wine. The few dance floors were at hillbilly honky-tonks on the edge of town. Marijuana and heroin, though more plentiful in El Paso than elsewhere in the U.S., was costly. Strippers couldn't uncover much. Whores had to be found through bellhops and taxi drivers.

But in Juárez …

When you crossed the Santa Fe Street Bridge over the Rio Grande, you emerged onto Avenida Juárez, the city's main tourist trap. In daylight, the main business there was "curios," the cheap, useless crap that American tourists can't go home without: fake silver-and-turquoise jewelry, straw sombreros, velvet paintings of bullfighters and flamenco dancers, salt-and-pepper shakers with "Souvenir of Old Mexico" on them, garish serapes, shoddy leather purses and wallets adorned with the Aztec calendar. Pitchmen stood at shop doors, tugging tourists' sleeves. "Hey, mister, step inside! Buy your lady a diamond! See it to believe it!"

But as the sun went down, the spiels turned seductive, urgent. "Hey, señores! Take a look! Naked blondes!" Avenida Juárez morphed into a sleazy Cinderella decked in neon, beckoning gullible Americans into the Crystal Palace, El Rancho Escondido and the Tivoli with their big bands and tuxedoed emcees and dirty jokes, or up dark and stinking stairs to raw sex shows in ratty dives.

On side streets where lights were sparse and dim were the real brothels, their names, too raunchy to print here, advertised in flyspecked, sputtering neon above their doors.

And drugs. All you had to do was ask.

People got murdered in Juárez. A hard rain or a coyote would uncover a shallow grave in the desert south of town. An American tourist would wind up naked with his throat cut, a victim of wandering into the wrong section of Juárez alone and in the dark. A bloated floater would be lifted from the river.

Since I could use the big Speed Graphic camera, Engledow sometimes sent me to Juárez to see what I could find about the latest dead, get quotes from the police and shoot a few pictures. My photos were of cops investigating, witnesses pointing and the like. The *Times* didn't want pictures of the grisly remains. But the Juárez papers did. Sometimes the entire top half of a front page would be a close-up photograph of a corpse. Sometimes it was printed in red ink.

I met Juárez reporters and photographers at these scenes. One became a friend. He was Hector Padilla, a reporter for *El Fronterizo*. He looked like a Mexican movie star – wavy hair; sexy mustache, loads of Latin charm – and he was well connected in Juárez. He knew the cops, politicians, rich businessmen, major pimps, everybody.

Hector and I made a pact: If he knew a hot story happening in Juárez, he would call me with the lowdown. If I knew one happening in El Paso, I would call him. We gave each other names and phone numbers. These were always stories about dead bodies.

Our pact had a second part, too.

Working for the *Times* had one perk: free movie passes. Theater managers brought small stacks of them to the newsroom each week and gave them to Mr. Latham, who locked them in his desk. If you approached him humbly and asked politely, he would give you a pair, but only once a week, like a stern father handing over an undeserving child's allowance.

Hector loved American movies. About once a month I gave him my passes to the Plaza, the big downtown picture palace. He could simply have bought tickets, of course, but entering the Plaza on a free pass was special to him. In return, he gave me shady-side tickets to the bullfights. He used his connections to get me membership in the rooftop swim club at Hotel Monte Carlo, near the big new bullring, Plaza Monumental. My friends and I would go there and have a drink after the bullfights, waiting for the traffic to thin.

Through a cousin who worked somewhere in the Mexican government bureaucracy, Hector even got me a Chihuahua fishing license.

Giving me this gift made him especially happy. But I never went fishing.

# SECTION I

## ROSA

El Paso Times
STRIKE!

The union at the copper smelter down by the river went on an illegal strike. Union leaders called the walkout because of some internal political rivalry, and the rank-and-file workers had nothing to gain by its outcome. They were just out of work.

Many workers lived in the adobe slum between the smelter and the river, called Smeltertown. They were poor. They had wives and children. When some workers defied the union leaders and tried to go to work, picketers attacked their cars with rocks and clubs.

The following Sunday, a heavy rain was falling, a rare sight in El Paso. When I arrived for work, Engledow was standing at an open window, watching the rain, smelling it. He said, "Come here, son."

I joined him at the window.

"Grab your camera and go see what's happening on the picket line," he said.

"In this?" I whined. "I'll get soaked! Nobody's going to picket in this!"

Engledow said, "Get your ass out there and don't come back till you've got the story."

I had my own car now, a two-tone-green 1955 Ford Fairlane with white-sidewall tires. I loved it. I wasn't about to risk it among a mob of club-swinging strikers. I called a taxi.

The driver stopped in front of the smelter gate. A single picketer stood there, holding a sign. He wore a soggy serape and a big straw sombrero like the ones that tourists bought in Juárez. The rain had destroyed its shape, and its wide brim drooped around the man's thin face.

On the other side of the road, a dozen cars were parked in a row, facing the gate. Each car held three or four strikers.

"Wait for me," I told the cabdriver.

"No," he said. "Pay me."

He made a quick U-turn and was gone. I was in the middle of the road, holding my Speed Graphic, my notebook and an Army-surplus bag of flashbulbs and film holders. Quickly, I was wet as the picketer.

I shot a picture of him. "What's this strike about?" I asked him, trying to sound casual.

He said nothing. He stared past my face.

"How long have you been standing in this rain?

No reply.

I had no way to get back to the *Times*, no way to call Engledow. So I stood in the road, trying to protect my camera with my drenched sports coat.

The driver in one of the cars across the road opened his door, got halfway out and waved. He was motioning me toward him. He was burly and had a big mustache and wore a brown felt hat. He looked like Pancho Villa. Three men were in the car with him. I was scared, but I went to the car.

"Get out of the rain," the man said. He told the man in the front passenger seat to move to the back. I climbed in beside the driver. "What you doing out here?" he asked.

"I'm a reporter. From the *Times.*"

"Yeah, I figured. Because of the camera."

"My name is Bryan Woolley." I stuck out my hand. The driver shook it. "Rudy Gonzales," he said. He introduced the other three men. I shook hands with them all.

They started talking about the strike. They didn't like it. They couldn't feed their families. Their union bosses were no good. Slowly, I relaxed. These weren't thugs. No clubs were hidden under their seats. They were getting a raw deal, and it was hurting them. I wanted to take notes, but was afraid they would stop talking if I opened my notebook. I just listened. We had been sitting maybe half an hour, quietly talking, gazing through the rain-streaked windshield at the miserable picketer across the road, when Rudy told me about Rosa.

She was his daughter. She was 9 years old, a beautiful girl. She was a victim of polio and wore steel braces on her legs. She had outgrown the braces and needed new ones, but Rudy didn't have the money to buy them. If the strike didn't end soon, who knew when he could save enough? His voice was full of love and sorrow.

I cleared my throat. "Rudy," I said quietly, "may I take a picture of Rosa?"

Rudy didn't answer. He started the car and steered it through the rain to Smeltertown, to one of the adobe shacks. We all got out. A face, Rudy's wife's, appeared behind the screen door. She opened it and invited us in.

Rosa was sitting in the sparsely furnished living room. She smiled big when she saw her father. She seemed to light up the room and the whole gloomy afternoon. Rudy lifted her from the chair, sat down and set her on his lap. Rudy's wife made us coffee. We talked.

Finally I asked, "May I take the picture?"

Rudy told his wife what I wanted. She didn't want to be in a picture, she said. She didn't like the way she was dressed.

I shot a picture of Rudy kneeling, buckling the braces on Rosa's legs. Rosa was smiling shyly into my lens.

Rudy and his companions gave me a ride to the *Times.* I wrote the story and developed the picture. Engledow put them in the middle of Page One.

Next afternoon, an anonymous caller told Engledow that if I returned to the picket line, something bad would happen to me. It didn't matter. Two days after the story ran, the smelter workers refused to picket anymore. In defiance of the union politicos, they went to work.

I end this little collection of memories with Rudy and Rosa because theirs was the best story I ever did for the *Times.* And it taught me the power of the word. It taught me that telling the truth in a newspaper can do more good than you expect.

Meanwhile, I was engaged to my high school sweetheart. She told me that a reporter wasn't a respectable thing to be and she wouldn't marry me unless I entered another vocation. This, I later learned, was really her mother speaking, but I agreed to it. In August 1958 I turned 21, she turned 18, I graduated from Texas Western College, I quit my job and we married.

Engledow was deeply hurt, I think. He had given me the big break that I was throwing away. I was full of grief.

Over nine years, I taught high school English, worked as a bank teller, did manual labor on a seismograph crew, spent six years in two graduate schools and edited a church magazine for teenagers.

Then the marriage ended and I got a job as night correspondent in the Tulsa Bureau of The Associated Press. At last I was back where I had always belonged. For nearly half a century, the wonderful room has been my home.

## ABOUT THE AUTHOR

**Bryan Woolley's** wonderful room wasn't always in Texas. During the 1960s, after several unsatisfying non-newspaper jobs and six years of graduate school at Texas Christian University and Harvard, he served a short time as an Associated Press correspondent in Tulsa, Oklahoma, then as city editor of *The Anniston Star* in Alabama. In 1969 he joined *The Courier-Journal* in Louisville, Kentucky, and wrote there for seven years. In 1976 he moved to *The Dallas Times Herald,* and in 1989 to *The Dallas Morning News,* where he worked until his retirement in 2006. In addition to several collections of his best newspaper work, he has published four novels and two children's books.

Woolley is the recipient of numerous honors for his writing, including the PEN West Literary Journalism Award; three Stanley Walker Newspaper Journalism Awards and one O. Henry Magazine Journalism Award (from the Texas Institute of Letters); four Texas Headliner Journalism Awards; and the Spur Award for Best Historical Novel from the Western Writers of America.

He lives in Dallas with his wife, the poet Isabel Nathaniel. He has two grown, married sons and two granddaughters. Over the years, he has written about them all.

**Wings Press** was founded in 1975 by Joanie Whitebird and Joseph F. Lomax, both deceased, as "an informal association of artists and cultural mythologists dedicated to the preservation of the literature of the nation of Texas." Publisher, editor and designer since 1995, Bryce Milligan is honored to carry on and expand that mission to include the finest in American writing—meaning *all* of the Americas, without commercial considerations clouding the choice to publish or not to publish.

Wings Press attempts to produce multicultural books, chapbooks, CDs and ebooks that, we hope, enlighten the human spirit and enliven the mind. We believe that writing is a transformational art form capable of changing the world, primarily by allowing us to glimpse something of each other's souls. Good writing is innovative, insightful, and interesting. But most of all it is honest.

Likewise, Wings Press is committed to treating the planet itself as a partner. Thus the press uses as much recycled material as possible, from the paper on which the books are printed to the boxes in which they are shipped.

As Robert Dana wrote in *Against the Grain*, "Small press publishing is personal publishing. In essence, it's a matter of personal vision, personal taste and courage, and personal friendships." Welcome to our world.

Colophon

This first edition of *The Wonderful Room*, by Bryan Woolley, has been printed on 55 pound Edwards Brothers Natural Paper containing a high percentage of recycled fiber. Book and section titles have been set in "PaintPeel" type, the text in Adobe Caslon type. All Wings Press books are designed and produced by Bryce Milligan.

On-line catalogue and ordering available at www.wingspress.com

Wings Press titles are distributed to the trade by the Independent Publishers Group www.ipgbook.com and in Europe by www.gazellebookservices.co.uk